Gracie's Ears

Written and Illustrated by Debbie Blackington

PEBBLETON PRESS

Inquiries should be addressed to
Pebbleton Press
P.O. Box 1894
Duxbury, MA 02331
or www.pebbletonpress.com.

Printed in the United States of America.
ISBN 978-0-976001-19-5

For my Gracie with love, and for Gracies everywhere.

When Gracie was adopted, we had
no idea that she had hearing difficulties.
We hope this book helps introduce what hearing aids are
and what a difference they can make to those who wear them.

Special thanks to Traci Ruiz who helped get us home!
Thank you to everyone in the Otolaryngology Department of Children's Hospital in Boston and Waltham;
and the Northeastern University Guild.
Additional thanks to Brynne and Gracie, as well as other family and friends who gave creative feedback to our story.

When Gracie wakes up, she wiggles her toes.

She looks with her eyes.

She smells with her nose...

 but Gracie's ears are sleeping.

She puts on her clothes, then comes down to eat.

She brushes her hair

and slips shoes on her feet.

She goes off to school, where she runs out to play.

But when her friends talk, she can't hear what they say
...because Gracie's ears are sleeping.

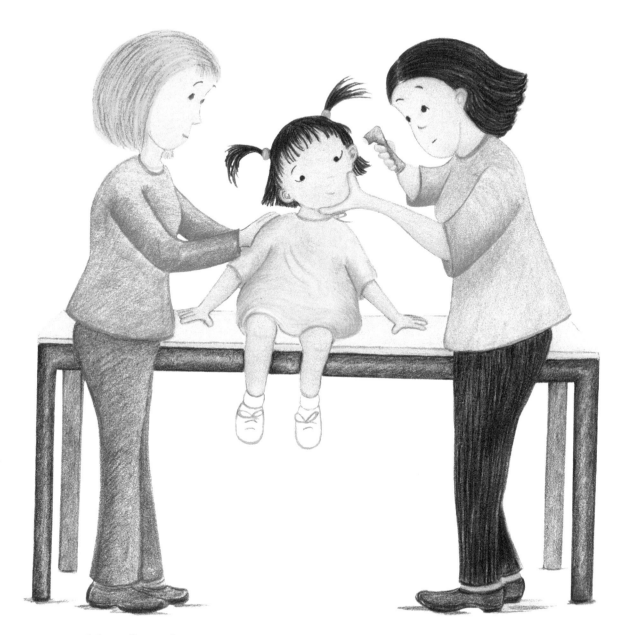

Her family went to doctors and hospitals too.

They searched for some answers to know what to do to help Gracie's ears stop sleeping.

Then, earphones were placed on her head
to play beeping sound games until doctors said,
"We can help Gracie's ears stop sleeping."

"Gracie needs hearing aids to help her hear,
made just for her to fit in each ear."

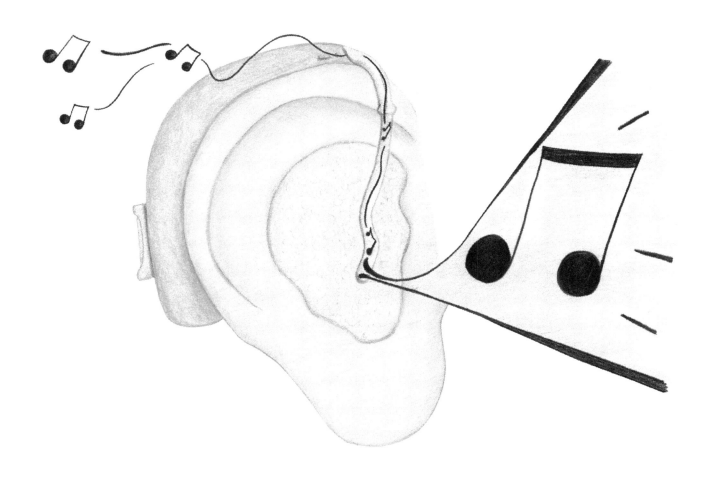

"Hearing aids make sounds louder.
They help push the sound through,
to have Gracie's ears work like most people's do.
This will make Gracie's ears stop sleeping."

Molds were made of her ears with special
hearing aid goop.

She got to pick colors from any group.

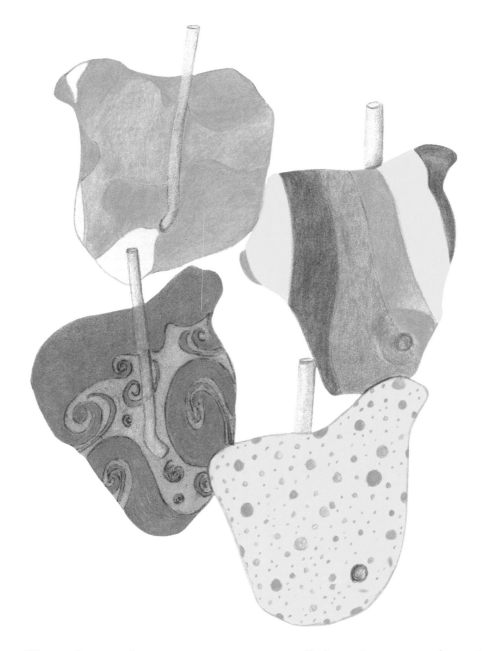

She chose between spots, wild stripes and swirls.

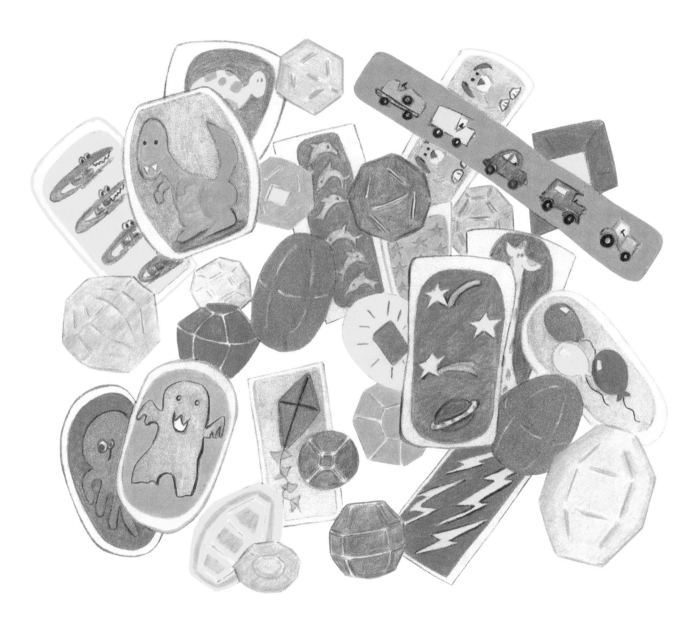

There were stickers for boys, jewels for girls.

At last they were done. Now, the very best part.

When she put them on...would her ears start?

Gracie's eyes got large. Her mouth was agape.
Sounds whooshed through her hearing aids.
Gracie's ears were awake!

She could hear
her friends laugh!

She could hear the birds sing!

She could hear car horns beep!
She could hear the phone ring!

Everyone was so happy that Gracie could hear,
with swirled orange-pink-white hearing aids
she had in each ear.

Now when Gracie wakes up, she wiggles her toes.

She looks with her eyes.

She smells with her nose.

Then she gets her hearing aids and puts one in each ear.

She smiles a big smile because...

Gracie can hear.

Printed in the USA
CPSIA information can be obtained
at www.ICGtesting.com
LVHW071938110224
771548LV00003B/5